This Is
Not a Cookbook

این یک کتاب آشپزی نیست

ROXANA
MANOUCHEHRI

skein
press

First published in 2025 by Skein Press
skeinpress.com

Design and layout by Wayne Kehoe – *waynekehoe.com*
Typeset in Bressay and Bressay Arabic by Dalton Maag
Printed by Henry Ling Limited, at the Dorset Press, Dorchester

ISBN 978-1-915017-06-2

The author would like to express her appreciation to the team at Skein Press
for their support over the past two years in the process of completing this book.

Skein Press gratefully acknowledges the financial support it receives
from The Arts Council of Ireland and The Rowan Trust.

the arts council chomhairle ealaíon | funding literature

The Rowan Trust

Contents

In 2008, I made a large-scale painting titled *This is not the last supper*, inspired by Leonardo da Vinci's *The Last Supper* (c. 1495–98). In my version, I changed the original artwork to reflect the playfulness often incorporated in traditional Persian paintings. My approach to *This Is Not a Cookbook* is the same; the recipes are my own versions, flavoured by my experiences travelling and living in different countries. Food is a wonderful tool to break down the barriers between different cultures. Sharing food reminds us that, at heart, we are all the same.

Food is a form of conceptual art. The tastes, smells, colours and shapes of different dishes and ingredients evoke memories, thoughts and dreams. We grow up eating the food made by our grandparents or parents, and the culture of food plays a big part in shaping our characters. Many of us associate particular foods from our childhood with warm feelings and good, or occasionally sad, memories. Food ties us to our families and traditions, holding a special and personal value for each of us.

When I started working on *This Is Not a Cookbook*, I was searching for my identity as an immigrant artist in Ireland. I had just moved to Ireland from South Korea. The importance of food in Korean culture is undeniable. All artistic, intellectual and political conversations take place around a round table covered with colourful little bowls filled with local specialties. Visiting some Korean *ajumas* (older ladies) in their houses to learn the secrets of their delicious food, I became deeply involved with the relationship between food and art.

This Is Not a Cookbook is a collection of easy recipes presented in an unusual way. Each recipe sits alongside a short vignette drawn from my memories, sometimes uplifting, sometimes nostalgic, sometimes sad. I drew all the images accompanying the text by hand, using the technique of lino printing, inspired by lithographs from the Qajar period in Iran. The scenes depicted there are often innocent and simple, full of life and joy. The decorative patterns and motifs in the margins of these manuscripts are beautiful and can be found in many kinds of old manuscripts around the world. Trying to find the connection between Irish and Iranian culture, for me, was at the core of writing and illustrating this book.

The book is about the life of an artist, originally Persian and officially
Irish, who is trying to place her identity in Ireland, in a place which, for
the past 15 years, she has called home. These memories are drawn from
my childhood, growing up during the Iran–Iraq war. I never imagined
that someday in the future I would witness the same thing happening
to so many people around the world, that war between countries would
continue and many more children would suffer. It is my hope that the
beautiful tastes, sights and smells of the food that we share might, in
some small way, bring us together and ease our passage through these
hard times.

Shami

شامی

SHAMI *reminds me of my grandmother, my mum's mother, Malak Taj Khanoom. She was a master at making* shami, *which is a kind of kotlet or kebab in Iran, usually containing beans and meat. It's dry, so it needs to be served with a sauce. There are many different kinds of* shami *in Persian cuisine.*

Malak Taj, or Maman Malak as we called her, was a great cook. Her kitchen smelled like butter and sugar – warm, delicious and cosy. It was a tiny room – two people could barely fit in it – but she made the most delicious food there. Her father was from Ghafghaz and her cooking was influenced by Azeri and Russian cuisine. *Kotlet*, *dolmeh*, Olivier salad and *piroshki* were everyday foods in her house. My family used to visit her once a week. We would spend the whole day in that beautiful old house, with lunch tenderly cooked by Grandma. In the evening, my dad would collect us on his way home from work.

Maman Malak lived in a typical, traditional Qajar-style house in Tehran, called *panj dari* or *hasht dari*, meaning a garden surrounded by five or eight doors. Her house had a small garden, with rooms arranged in a semi-circular shape around it, each with large wooden windows. In the middle of the garden was a *hoz* حوض which was a little pool with a fountain, often with goldfish, very common in traditional Persian houses. The little ponds are decorative but they also keep the gardens cool during the hot summers. I used to wish the *hoz* was bigger so we could swim in it. After the Persian New Year ceremony, we would leave our goldfish in Maman Malak's *hoz* as a tradition. My grandma would soak watermelons in it to keep them cool for my dad. When he came to collect us, he would sit down and enjoy some cold watermelon.

In wintertime there was a *korsi* کرسی in one of the rooms. My grandma would make the *korsi* by putting an electric heater under the large, low, heavy wooden coffee table and covering it with a beautiful blanket. The table would be covered in small plates and bowls filled with nuts, sweets and dried fruits. In the corner of the room there was a *samovar* and tea was always available. As kids, we loved this traditional way of keeping our feet cosy and warm while sitting with family for snacks and chats. I remember tucking my legs under the table, feeling the weight of the heavy blanket and listening to my grandma telling us stories.

Maman Malak loved birds and kept hens and turkeys in her garden. I was scared of the hens, who chased me, but I loved to play with them when they were little chicks. In one corner of the garden there was a narrow staircase that led deep down into the ground. At the bottom of those stairs was the *hammam* حمام, which is the traditional style shower room in Iran, Turkey and some other countries. The *hammam* was dark and damp, and I was too scared to go there on my own. In another corner of the garden was the toilet. It was very tough to leave the warm house and *korsi* to go to the toilet in the cold of winter.

The best part about spending time in Maman Malak's house was when the adults were having a nap after lunch. There were two little rooms to the side of the main entrance where we could go and have a look from the windows. My sisters and I used to sneak into the kitchen and take some cold *shami* to the garden to eat as snacks while we played with the birds or the goldfish in the *hoz* and wandered around the different corners of the garden.

I lost Maman Malak nearly 20 years ago, before I moved to Ireland. I think about her often, about how proud she was to be from Tehran and all her beautiful stories from before the Islamic Revolution, stories which sounded like fairytales to me and my sisters. *Shami* was her special dish, and I loved it. I try to make it as well as my grandmother, but there must have been something about that house and her kitchen that created the magic. I can't find it here in Dublin.

Shami

This is my version of *shami*, in memory of Maman Malak.

Makes 9 medium-sized shami kebabs

INGREDIENTS

FOR THE SHAMI

- 200g yellow lentils
- A bunch of fresh parsley
- 1 medium onion
- 5 garlic cloves
- 250g minced lamb
- 1 tsp cumin
- 1 tbsp turmeric
- 1 tbsp sumac
- 4 tbsp breadcrumbs
- 2 eggs
- 2 tbsp wholemeal flour

FOR THE SAUCE

- 3 tbsp pomegranate paste (You can find pomegranate paste in Middle Eastern supermarkets. I recommend Persian brands as other brands tend to be much sweeter.)
- 2 tbsp tomato purée
- The juice of 1 lime
- Salt and pepper
- 50g butter

METHOD

- Soak the yellow lentils for at least 6 hours, changing the water a few times.
- In a food processor, blend the soaked yellow lentils and parsley.
- Peel and grate the onion and garlic cloves, using a fine sieve to strain away the onion juice.
- Put these mixtures in a large bowl and add the spices. Using your hands, mix well.
- Refrigerate the mixture for 20 minutes.
- Using the refrigerated mixture, roll balls a bit smaller than a ping pong ball.
- Cover the bottom of a shallow dish or tray with the breadcrumbs. Lay the balls out on the tray and flatten them with your palm. Make a hole in the centre of each one with your finger to create rings, so they look kind of like thick CDs. Lightly press the breadcrumbs into each side of the rings.
- Pan fry the *shami* on low to medium heat on both sides until golden brown. I use coconut oil mixed with ghee for frying. You can use olive oil if you prefer.
- To make the sauce, add all the ingredients to a small saucepan and heat over a low heat for 10 minutes, stirring regularly.
- Pour the sauce over the balls.

Serve with a green salad and flatbread.

Fish Kotlet

كتلت ماهى

IN IRAN, *seafood comes from the Caspian Sea in the north and from the Persian Gulf in the south. There is a huge selection of sea fruits and fish available, and I have always wondered why Iranian people don't eat more fish. Other than for the Persian New Year dinner, when it is a tradition to eat fish, it is not eaten as much as lamb or beef.*

In Tehran, the area where you lived determined where you could go to school. Most of the children in the Maryam Institute, the private French school I attended, were from the same social and cultural background. When the Iran–Iraq war broke out, life changed dramatically. All the private schools closed down. I was seven years old when I had to move to a new school. The Maryam Institute, where I had dreamed of ending up at a Paris university, was gone.

The dark blue hijab I had to wear to my new school was so long I could wrap my whole body in it. I didn't know how to fix it around my head. I had never worn a hijab before. Fortunately, we could take it off when we were in the classroom. All the students and teachers in the school were female.

People affected by the war in the south of Iran had to leave their land and houses to move to Tehran. In my class, there were some kids from the south. We called them *jang zadeh* جنگ زده, meaning 'war-torn'. Their accent was different from ours.

One of the *jang zadeh* girls was especially sweet and kind, with blonde hair and blue eyes and a constant generous smile. Her name was Nooshin. She had a beautiful voice and would drum on the wooden classroom desks with her fingers in magical ways. The rhythms she played were from the south and she sang *bandari* بندری songs. *Bandar* means 'port' in Farsi and *bandari* tunes belong to the south of Iran. They are usually very energetic and up-tempo, perfect for dancing.

We were all curious about life in the south of Iran. I had heard from my parents that in the Shah's time, southern cities were popular among international tourists, with their sunny beaches, white villas and tall palm trees along the Persian Gulf. When Nooshin talked about her hometown, her eyes sparkled with excitement and tears and we all gathered around her, listening to her magical stories about that beautiful happy town.

The *jang zadeh* families who didn't have relatives in Tehran had to stay in abandoned buildings. There was one massive old hotel, not far from our house in a busy, polluted part of town which was a hub for buses and taxis. The building was in very poor condition. Its walls were of dirty concrete stained with old graffiti of the Supreme Leader's face, a burnt American flag, and statements about continuing the war till the last breath. We could see clotheslines dangling in the windows. Nooshin told us that she didn't have a bed. There were too many families with young children staying there, so they slept on the floors. There were just a few bathrooms and shower rooms, not enough for everyone. I wondered how she was always so cheerful, never complaining.

One day, Nooshin brought in a fish *kotlet* her mum had made for us to try. I still remember its sour and spicy taste. She told us about the barbecued seafood, sardines and anchovies, sold as street food in the south. They would catch fresh fish from the sea, roast it on an open fire on the beach and eat it while the street musicians sang and played the *nay anban* (an instrument much like the bagpipes) and danced at night.

Most *jang zadeh* people never went back to the south. It took many years to rebuild the destroyed towns, buildings, farms and factories. Some places have never fully recovered.

Later, when I moved to Ireland, the music of the uilleann pipes and bagpipes would remind me of *nay anban* and the south of Iran. I make fish *kotlet* often and I always think of Nooshin when I do.

Fish Kotlet

I created this recipe for my mum to encourage her to eat fish.
I tried to make sure she wouldn't smell the sea or see the shape of the fish.

Serves 4

INGREDIENTS – FOR THE KOTLET

- 2 medium rooster potatoes
- 2 cod fillets
- 3 garlic cloves
- A few bay leaves
- 1 medium onion
- 1 tsp turmeric
- 2 tsp dried or 2 tbsp chopped fresh coriander
- 2 tbsp dried lime powder (if you can't find lime powder, you can use the zest of 2 limes with the juice of 1 or 2 mashed slices of lemon confit)
- 3 tbsp flour (any kind of flour works – I use semolina)
- 2 eggs
- 250–300ml milk (full fat or low fat)
- 5 tbsp breadcrumbs
- Salt and pepper

FOR THE TAMARIND SAUCE

- 150g tamarind
- 1 tbsp tomato purée
- 1 tsp cornflour
- 1 tsp hot chilli powder
- 1 tbsp sugar
- 50g butter or ghee (or you can use olive oil or coconut oil)

METHOD – FISH KOTLET

- Boil the potatoes until they are cooked through. Then drain and set aside to cool.
- Put the cod fillets in a medium saucepan with the garlic cloves, a bay leaf and a pinch of salt. Cover with cold water and bring to the boil. Reduce the heat and simmer for 5 minutes. Remove the fish and garlic from the water and set aside to cool. (If you don't like the smell of fish, you can use milk as a cooking liquid instead of water.)
- After the potatoes have cooled a little, mash them in a large mixing bowl.
- When the fish has cooled, remove the skin and bones.
- Place a fine sieve in a bowl and grate the onion over the sieve, getting rid of as much of the juice as possible.
- Add the turmeric, coriander, dried lime powder and 1 tablespoon of the flour. Season with salt and pepper. Mix well.
- Add the eggs and, using your hands, mix well.
- Cover and refrigerate the mixture for 30 minutes.
- On a baking tray, spread the remaining 2 tablespoons of flour and a handful of breadcrumbs.
- Using the refrigerated fish and potato mixture, make ping pong-sized fish balls and roll each ball in the breadcrumb and flour mixture until it is well coated. This amount should make around 8 balls.
- Fry the balls on a non-stick frying pan over a medium heat. (I use ghee for frying, which adds great flavour.)

TAMARIND SAUCE

- Fill a large cup or small bowl with boiling water and allow the tamarind to soak for 1 hour to let all the juice seep out.
- Use a sieve to remove the seeds from the dissolved tamarind, leaving a watery, light-brown liquid.
- Add the liquid to a small pan and stir. Cook over a low to medium heat for about 10 minutes
- Add the tomato purée and cornflour and stir well. When the mixture starts to thicken, turn off the heat.
- Add ghee or butter, stir well and add pepper, sugar and salt if needed.

Serve with tortillas and sour cream.

Tahdig

ته دیگ

Tʜᴅɪɢ ته دیگ *is a Farsi word meaning 'the bottom of the pot'. Iranians eat rice nearly every day – it's a staple food for us. There are different kinds of* tahdig, *with crispy rice, rice and herbs, lettuce leaves, potatoes or flatbread at the bottom of the pot, with some butter, ghee or vegetable oil. At family gatherings everyone fights to get a piece of the* tahdig.

It was early afternoon on a sunny summer day in Tehran. My mother's sister and her family were invited to dinner and we three girls were helping to clean the house. The air was full of the smell of fenugreek from the Persian stew, *ghormeh sabzi* قورمه سبزی, Mum was cooking. The stew needs to cook slowly, and she had been preparing it since the morning.

Most of my mum's family had moved abroad after the Islamic Revolution and had settled in California and Sweden. One sister and a brother were the only ones still living in Tehran, and though my mum was close to her sister, she did not keep in touch with her brother. I liked my aunt very much. She was a hard-working woman, strong and centred. Her husband was very kind to my sisters and me and would take us to movies and on picnics. They had three children, two sons and one daughter, and my family and theirs travelled together every year to the Caspian Sea. Only their daughter was coming to dinner with them that day. She had just returned from Bangalore after her studies in accountancy. Their older son was studying at a university in Isfahan, and the younger son, just 21, was fighting in the war. I had heard my parents talking and knew my aunt hadn't wanted her young boy to go to war, but her husband didn't stop him. They had many arguments about it. My cousin had been badly injured once in the war, but after a few months of recovery he went back to the frontline to fight. He was somewhere in the south of Iran in one of the combat zones.

The rice was still cooking on the stove when the phone rang. My mum answered and her face grew fearful as she talked. Then she went to her bedroom and asked my dad to follow. After a few minutes, they came out of the room, both looking distressed. My mum had dressed in a hurry in a black *mantu* and white scarf, without make-up. I asked who had been on the phone and where they were going. It was clear she didn't want to give us much information.

'It was your uncle on the phone. He has some bad news about your cousin. But we don't know what exactly happened.'

I knew my mum and her brother didn't talk often and I was scared.

As my parents left the house, my mum instructed me to turn off the rice pot at seven o'clock so there would be a nice crispy *tahdig* at the bottom of the pot. She said to stay calm and offer the visitors tea when they came.

Our guests arrived around six o'clock, happy and cheerful. My pretty cousin was wearing a dark blue dress and red lipstick. We kissed and hugged each other, and we tried to behave normally.

'Where are your parents?' my aunt asked suspiciously.

'They had to buy something. They'll be home soon,' I said nervously, avoiding eye contact.

My older sister served them tea as they sat in the kitchen. After about an hour we were still waiting for my parents to return. My aunt kept asking, 'Where are they? Has something bad happened?' Her husband paced up and down the garden.

A while later my mum came through the door with her brother, my dad and two bearded strangers. They all walked straight out to the garden.

My aunt ran after them shouting furiously, 'Is it about my son?' Then she sat on the ground desperately curling into herself, saying, 'I knew, I knew.'

The bearded men gave my cousin's metal dog tag to my aunt and said they were sorry.

'Tell me he is not dead!' my aunt repeated over and over.

'Did you see him? Did you see his body? Are you sure it was him?' she asked, turning to my mum.

My aunt's husband ran towards one of the bearded men and hit him hard, shouting and cursing, threatening to kill him, while my dad tried to hold him back.

We covered our ears. The screaming seemed like it would never stop. I could feel tears running down my cheeks. The smell of burnt rice, the sound of screams and cries reverberated. Finally, I crept out to the kitchen and turned off the stove.

We didn't have dinner that night.

Tahdig

In Iran we use long grain rice to make *tahdig*. The smoked rice comes from the north of Iran and the Caspian Sea. It is the best quality rice according to Iranian people. In Dublin, I buy Persian rice from an Afghan supermarket on Capel Street.

Another important ingredient in Persian rice dishes is saffron. The best quality saffron comes from Iran, the Khorasan province and, of course, Afghanistan. We use it in nearly every dish. I have heard that consuming saffron makes you happy. And if you go to a Persian restaurant, you should definitely try some saffron ice cream.

Serves 4

INGREDIENTS

- 400g long grain rice (if you don't have long grain, you can use Basmati)
- 2 tbsp salt
- 1/4 tsp saffron
- 1 tbsp vegetable oil
- 100g butter, melted

METHOD

- Wash the rice to remove any dirt and starch. When the water runs clear, cover the rice with water and add the salt. Leave to soak for 2 hours.
- Grind the saffron using a pestle and mortar.
- To a small bowl, add 2 tablespoons of hot water and add the ground saffron. Refrigerate for at least 30 minutes. This will bring out the beautiful colour of the saffron. Alternatively, after mixing the saffron and hot water, add 1/4 teaspoon sugar, stir and allow to stand for about 10 minutes.
- In a large non-stick saucepan, boil 1 litre water. Add the salted soaked rice to the boiling water and simmer for 5 to 7 minutes, depending on what kind of rice you are using, or until it's 1/3 of the way cooked.
- Drain the rice in a colander and run some cold water over it for about 1 minute. Let it stand.
- Return the saucepan to the stove. Over a medium heat, add the vegetable oil, half of the melted butter and a tiny bit of saffron.
- Return the rice to the pot and shape it into a little mountain. Wait 2 minutes and then add 1/2 cup hot water.
- Cover and cook for a few minutes. When you see vapour rising, lower the heat.
- In a small bowl, mix the rest of the melted butter and saffron with 1/2 cup of boiling water. Add this mixture to the rice.
- Wrap the saucepan lid in a clean cotton tea towel or a thick piece of kitchen towel and place on top of the saucepan. Cook for 40 minutes over a very low heat.
- After 40 minutes, turn off the heat and carefully take the saucepan to the sink and run cold water over the outside. You'll hear a beautiful hiss.
- Using a round tray, larger than your pot, flip the contents of the pot onto the tray and you will see the beautiful *tahdig* on top of the cooked rice.

Serve with *torshi* or Greek yoghurt.

Abgoosht

آب گوشت

AB MEANS *'water' and* goosht *means 'meat' in Farsi. Abgoosht, also called* dizy, *is like a Persian version of Irish stew – lamb mixed with vegetables and spices.*

One summer, when I was 12, my sisters and I went to stay with my grandmother at her holiday home in the countryside. In the darkness of those warm nights, I would sit on the ledge of a large window looking up at the sky full of bright stars. They seemed so close, close enough to touch. The only sounds were the crickets chirping and my grandma's footsteps as she walked around the house. I can still remember the scent in the air, a mixture of hay, fresh grass, clay and cowpat. I could have sat there forever.

My favourite part of the house was the ceiling. I used to stare at its sturdy wooden beams while I was in bed. The window frames were old and wooden and the walls were made of mud and straw. The largest room in the house looked out onto the street, where family and guests would gather in the evenings. There was a pantry attached, where my grandmother kept a large, antique, metal packing case full of dried fruits and nuts, packets of tea leaves, dried bread and candies.

A long, narrow terrace led to the second main room. In the corner was a large metal *samovar*, a traditional Persian-style oil-burner kettle for making tea, which was lit most of the time. The sound of boiling water and the smell of tea leaves and fresh milk are what I remember most from early-morning breakfasts. My grandma didn't do much baking or cooking. She would give us milk, yoghurt and fruits that she bought from the local markets instead.

Every afternoon, my sisters and I used to walk to my aunt's house. We had to use all our strength to open the big wooden latches on the entrance door, which was studded with decorative metal pins. It opened onto a narrow alley, with clay houses to one side and a waterway overgrown with wild greens on the other. We had to be careful not to get stung by wild nettles as we squeezed through. Sometimes we would bump into local people as we walked and we knew we should say hi to them. They all knew we were Mansour Khan's girls, and that made us feel proud.

All the land around my aunt's house belonged to my dad and his relatives. My dad's own plot was a wild garden full of apple trees, and he dreamed of building his own country house there someday. We had to pass through my dad's land to enter the backyard of my aunt's house. Her door was always open, and we would walk through and climb the metal staircase, enter the half-circle terrace and loudly announce our arrival. She would greet us with kisses.

One day that summer, my aunt and grandmother decided to sacrifice a sheep, which is a tradition from Abrahamic times. My sisters and I went to see the sheep, which was tied by a rope to one of the walnut trees. It was chubby and calm, slowly eating the grass. There was a large bucket full of water nearby for it to drink. It is a very important part of the ritual to give the animal some water before sacrificing it. When a local farmer arrived with a large knife, we went to the other side of the garden to avoid witnessing the slaughter. The smell of blood, stool and grass filled the air. From a distance, I could see the farmer skinning the carcass.

In a corner of her garden, my aunt was cutting herbs – basil, chives, cress, parsley, coriander and more – to have as a side dish with the abgoosht they were going to make with the sacrificial meat. I went to help her, trying not to think about the sheep.

It was very busy in my aunt's kitchen. My mum, grandmother, aunt and cousins were all there, preparing the lamb, fat, onions, chickpeas and potatoes. The stew would be left to simmer for hours, before being shared among the neighbours.

That evening, I helped set the plates and cutlery on a long *sofreh* on the floor. The dish was served with fresh herbs from the garden, raw onions, a yoghurt drink and flatbread. I didn't feel hungry at all. My parents and my aunt tried to convince me to try a bite of the *abgoosht*, but I refused and ate some bread with cheese and fresh herbs instead.

Years later, I tasted Irish stew for the first time. It reminded me of home, and I decided to make *abgoosht* in my own kitchen. With some small changes, I made the most delicious *abgoosht* for my guests and myself. It brought back memories of my grandmother and my eldest aunt, who are no longer alive, and my grandmother's house in the countryside, which no longer exists. I think about how delicious the food was, prepared with a sense of ritual and community, and how much more I appreciate it now that I am older and can better understand the significance of these traditions.

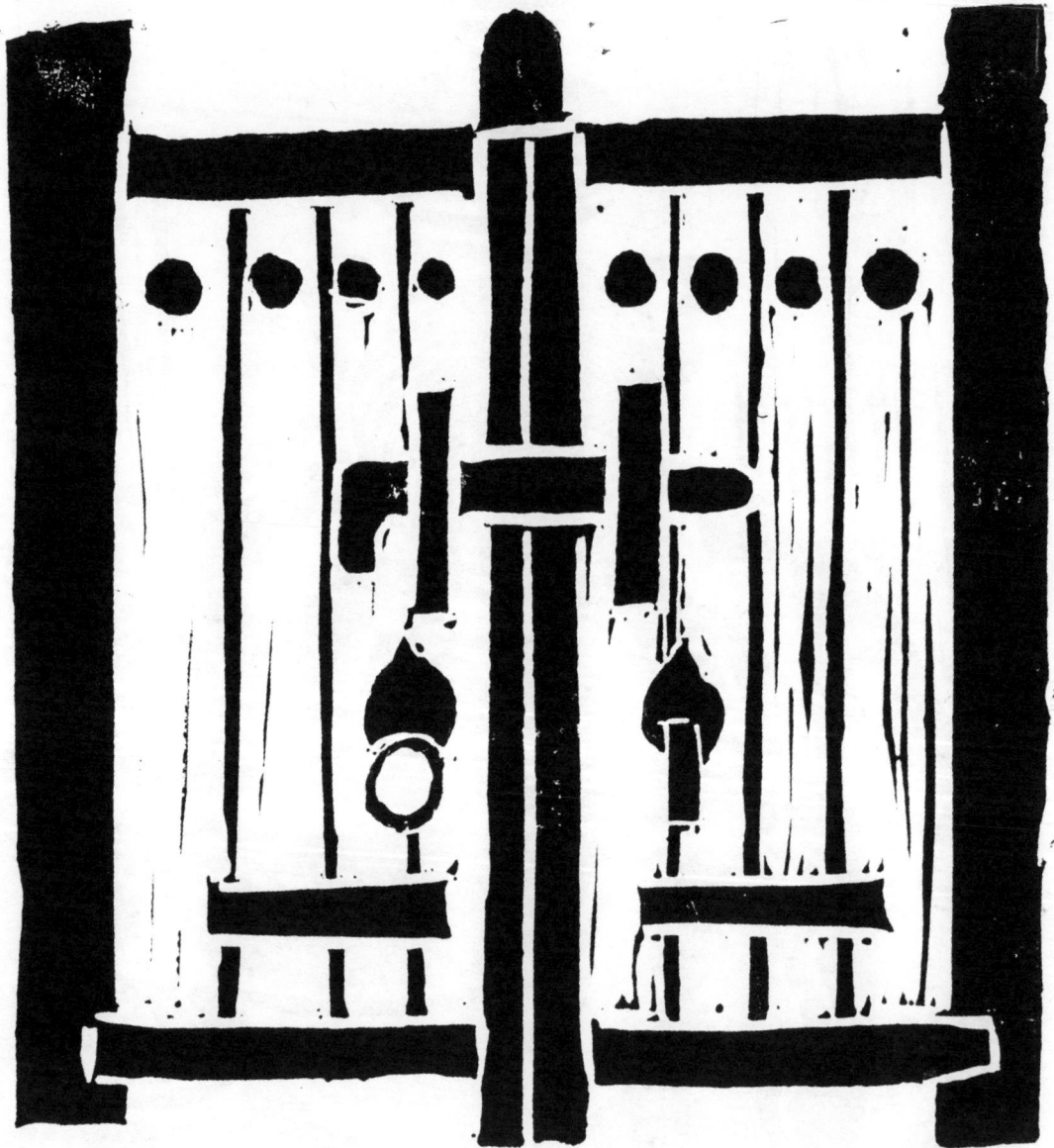

Abgoosht

Abgoosht is a traditional Iranian stew or broth. There are *dizy* houses (special restaurants that serve only *abgoosht*) in Iran. When I was younger, I didn't enjoy it, but I love it now and have made some adjustments to the original recipe.

Serves 4

INGREDIENTS

- 200g dried chickpeas
- 3 large white onions
- 2 tbsp ghee or 3 tbsp olive oil
- 500g good quality lamb shoulder or ribs
- 2 cinnamon sticks
- 2 bay leaves
- 1 tbsp tomato purée (I like to use pomegranate paste instead of tomato purée, but it can be hard to find if you don't have access to a Persian or Turkish supermarket)
- 4 large tomatoes or 1 tin chopped tomatoes
- 2 large potatoes,
- 1 tsp cardamom
- 1 tsp cinnamon powder
- 1 tsp turmeric
- 100g dried lime (if you can't find dried lime, you can use the juice of 4 fresh limes)
- 3 garlic cloves, finely chopped
- 1 tsp pepper
- 1 tsp salt
- 1 tsp thyme

METHOD

- Soak the chickpeas for 24 hours, changing the water a few times.
- Roughly chop the onions.
- In a large saucepan, heat 1 tablespoon of the ghee or oil. Add the chopped onions and sweat them until they are translucent.
- Cut the meat into cubes of about 3cm and add to the onions along with the rest of the ghee or oil.
- Over a medium heat, brown the meat on all sides.
- Add the bay leaves, cinnamon sticks and the finely chopped garlic.
- Add the tomato purée or pomegranate paste and stir.
- After 10 minutes, add 500ml of boiling water, or enough to cover the contents, and stir well.
- Lower the heat, put the lid on and allow to simmer gently for 30 minutes.
- After 30 minutes, add the soaked chickpeas.
- While the meat and chickpeas are cooking, chop the tomatoes and potatoes and add them in.
- Add the dried spices, thyme, salt, pepper and the dried lime.
- Allow the dish to cook very slowly, for a minimum of 2 hours over a low heat.
- Use a fork to check if the chickpeas and meat are thoroughly cooked. The meat should be soft, tender and juicy. Only a small amount of liquid should remain in the saucepan at this point.
- Using a sieve or a colander, decant the liquid – the soup element – into another saucepan. Now mash the chickpeas, meat and potatoes with a masher. We call this mixture *goosht koobideh* گوشت کوبیده, meaning mashed meat.
- You can serve the soup in bowls with pieces of dried flatbread soaking in it, or, alternatively, don't separate the liquid, and serve as a stew.

Serve the soup and the *goosht koobideh* with flatbread, fresh basil leaves and slices of raw onion. *Torshi* goes very well with *abgoosht*.

Torshi

ترشی

TORSHI *is a pickled side dish in Persian cuisine. My mum, like many other Persian women, used to make different kinds of torshi. Her speciality was* seer torshi سیر ترشی*, whole bulbs of garlic pickled with herbs and vinegar in a clean, airtight glass jar. It is an essential side dish on the Persian New Year's dinner table. In Iran all family houses have at least one jar of* seer torshi*. They say it should age like wine, the older the better. An old jar of* seer torshi *carries secrets and stories in families and also reminds me of how life can be short and unpredictable.*

It was a sunny day in early summer during the Iran–Iraq war. My younger sister and I were in the garden, ready to go to school. I was 11. We both had black *maghnae* on our heads, a special hijab we had to wear to school. The *maghnae* fully covered our hair, neck and shoulders, reaching our waists. I hated putting it on every morning, but I had to. The dark blue *mantu* and *maghnae* was the uniform of our school.

My sister was playing with kittens in the garden, but I was anxious about being late for school. I never liked cats, their noise and stretchy moves were annoying and unpleasant to me.

'Stop playing. We're late!'

'OK, just give me a few minutes to feed them,' my sister said, giving the kittens some leftover chicken bones from the previous night's dinner.

I looked at the *torshi* jars resting on the windowsills beside each other. There were too many. Who eats this much *torshi*? I asked myself.

Then I looked up at my grandmother's large windows on the second floor. My dad had taped all the windows with brown packing tape in X-shapes to prevent them from breaking from the vibrations of bombs and missiles. A few months previously, Iraq had started bombing Tehran. Before that the war was confined to the southern provinces of the country, around the Persian Gulf.

Suddenly the red siren sounded loudly, warning us that an air attack was about to happen and instructing us to leave our homes or places of work immediately and go to a shelter until we heard the white siren.

It was unusual to hear the siren in the morning. The sound was frightening, a warning sound, long and loud like a constant whistling, with a bass tone. We panicked. My mum ran to the garden, saying, 'Keep away from the windows!' We thought it was better to be in an open space rather than inside the house.

Everything happened so quickly. We were looking up at the sky when suddenly a huge red fireball came closer and closer, becoming larger, heading straight towards us. My sister and I hugged each other, shaking, I closed my eyes, pressing my eyelids together hard. Two seconds passed, and then the sound of an explosion. I was deaf for a few minutes. There was a whistling in my ears.

We were alive. We were sitting on the ground, covering our ears. Shards of broken glass were everywhere. The packing tape hadn't worked at all. Pieces of smelly brown garlic mixed with tiny bits of sharp, broken glass lay all around us. The smell of *seer torshi* would linger in our house for a long time after.

The missile had hit about 100 metres from our house. My parents, my grandmother and uncles went to the site. They didn't let us go with them in an effort to protect us from seeing the dead and our destroyed neighbourhood. We didn't go to school that day. My parents were in shock but thankful that the bomb hadn't hit us.

Days passed. My mum made more *seer torshi* and my dad taped my grandmother's windows with thicker, stronger packing tape.

Torshi

Torshi is a side dish of pickled vegetables eaten in Iran, Turkey, Greece, Arab countries, Mediterranean and Eastern European countries. Iranian people believe *torshi* helps digestion. I have tried many *torshi* recipes and finally came up with my very own version.

For this recipe, you'll need a sterilised 1 litre glass jar with an airtight lid, such as a Mason jar.

This recipe makes enough to fill a 1 litre jar

INGREDIENTS

- 1 medium carrot
- Green and red peppers (use 1 of each colour if they're small peppers and ½ of each if you're using bell peppers)
- 10 radishes
- 5 dried apricots
- A pinch of salt
- Chilli flakes to taste
- A bunch of fresh tarragon, chopped
- 1 tbsp dried marjoram
- 1 tbsp coriander seeds
- 5 garlic cloves
- 200ml or more apple cider vinegar (as much as you need to fill the jar)

METHOD

- Wash the carrots, peppers and radishes and dry them very carefully. We don't want even one drop of water in our *torshi* jar.
- On a very clean surface, julienne the carrots and peppers (i.e. cut them into matchsticks) and thinly slice the radishes.
- Peel the garlic cloves and pat dry with a paper towel to remove any moisture.
- Put the sliced vegetables and peeled garlic in a big mixing bowl and add the salt, chilli flakes, tarragon, marjoram and coriander seeds.
- Using a clean spoon, or just clean hands, transfer all the ingredients from the bowl to the jar and press them down with the spoon or your fingers.
- Pour in the apple cider vinegar to fill the jar. Wait 5 minutes for the vinegar to settle and then add some more until the jar is completely full.
- Close the lid and leave it in a dark corner. After a week your *torshi* will be ready, but it is like red wine – the longer you leave it, the tastier it will be.

Serve as a side dish with any kind of savoury meal, especially *kotlet*, *kebab* and mixed-rice dishes.

Piroshki

پیراشکی

PIROSHKI *comes from Russia and Eastern Europe, but it is a popular comfort food in Central Asia, Armenia and Iran, as well as among Iranian families with Russian, Armenian or Azeri roots. My grandmother and my mum were* piroshki *experts. I still remember the heavenly smell of fresh hot* piroshki *in my mum's kitchen when we were kids.*

On Tuesdays my mum would invite her best friends, Lily and Nooshi, over for their weekly art sessions. They would use the shower room as their studio. It was the biggest room in our house, very bright with a high ceiling and glass skylight in the roof. Lily was slim with blond hair and Nooshi was petite with dark hair. I liked them both and was fascinated by the stories of their childhood and the art school they all went to together. The only one who had continued her art practice professionally was Nooshi. She spent some time in Italy to advance her art studies and worked as a professional artist and children's book illustrator.

I remember the smell of oil paint and coffee on those Tuesdays. Lily, Nooshi and my mum would sit and chat with their tiny Armenian coffee cups upside down on paper towels. This ritual happened every single time they were together, drinking Armenian coffee and reading the dregs at the bottom of the cups. They often talked about the famous *piroshki* shop in the centre of Tehran, which they used to go to often. Later, when my mum started working, her office was close to that same *piroshki* shop. She would go there with her coworkers and then on to Café Naderi, a famous coffee shop popular among intellectuals in the Shah's time.

On those Tuesdays, the heavenly smell of *piroshki* batter would fill the air. My sisters and I, along with Nooshi and Lily's kids, couldn't wait to try a hot *piroshki* right out of the frying pan. My mum used to serve them with a nice homemade sauce, but I liked them better with ketchup.

Some of my favourite times with my mum were when she would show me her old photo albums. She had lots of pictures from her art school days, of her friends and herself in miniskirts, posing happily in Tehran's streets. I could hardly believe it was my mum dressed like that, walking around the streets freely, without having to worry about the moral police.

I knew the names of all her friends in the photos and had often listened to the stories about how they had scattered after the revolution. The only one who stayed in touch with mum, besides Nooshi and Lily, was an Armenian named Alvard who had married a Swiss man and now lived in Zurich. She visited Iran every few years, and the four old friends would gather together to have Armenian coffee. It was Alvard who had taught them coffee-cup reading, which is a tradition among Armenians. She was a master at making *piroshki*, which is also popular in Armenian cuisine.

Alvard's stays in Iran are always very short. The last time I met her was seven years ago, when I was in Tehran. We drank Armenian coffee and, this time, it was me who made *piroshki*, using my own recipe. My mum and her friends liked it a lot and in return I asked them all to have a look at my coffee cup. And we looked through the photo albums: my mum, Nooshi, Lily and Alvard in Tehran's parks, museums and streets during the Shah's time.

I make *piroshki* in my kitchen in Dublin and think of my mum. I close my eyes and can picture a sunny day and a sharp blue sky, four beautiful girls in short summer dresses with big hair walking and giggling in Tehran city centre. The Alborz Mountain, which can be seen from anywhere in the city, high and strong, stands on the north side. The girls buy hot *piroshkis* wrapped in brown paper in Khosravi, the famous *piroshki* shop, and eat them as they walk to Café Naderi. They order Armenian or Turkish coffee and sit sipping from the small cups, quietly chatting about their love lives and dreams for the future, waiting to read each others' cups.

Piroshki

This recipe makes about 10 piroshkis

INGREDIENTS

FOR THE DOUGH

- 150ml full-fat milk
- 1 (7g) sachet of instant yeast
- 1 tbsp granulated sugar
- 1 tsp salt
- 2 eggs
- 100g butter, melted
- 500g plain flour, and a little extra for dusting

FOR THE FILLING

- 1 tbsp olive oil
- 200g of any kind of minced meat of your choice (I use minced lamb, but vegetarians can replace the meat with mushrooms and spinach or any other vegetables)
- 1 tsp turmeric
- The juice of 1 fresh lime
- 2 tsp dried or 2 tbsp freshly chopped parsley
- 1 large onion, finely chopped
- 1 tbsp tomato purée
- Salt and pepper

METHOD

- Preheat the oven to 200°C/180°C fan.
- In a small saucepan over a medium heat, warm the milk (but don't boil it) and mix in the yeast, sugar and salt and stir well.
- Set the mixture aside for 10 minutes, then add the eggs and melted butter. Mix well to combine.
- Slowly add the flour, mixing at the same time. This part is much easier if someone helps you by adding the flour while you mix.
- Cover and leave the dough mixture in a warm, dark place for 1 hour.
- Meanwhile, make the filling. Heat the olive oil in a frying pan over a high heat and sauté the onions until they are translucent.
- Add the minced meat and turmeric and cook over a low heat for 10 minutes.
- Add the lime juice and parsley and cook for another 5 minutes.
- Dust some flour onto a flat, clean surface. Transfer the dough to the surface and knead for 5 minutes.
- Shape the dough into balls the size of ping pong balls – not too small as they will have a filling.
- Flatten the balls using a small plate, to create discs roughly 2mm in thickness.
- Using a teaspoon, put some filling in the middle of each disc of dough and fold over to create a half-moon shape. I use wet fingers and some pressure to secure the edges.
- Line a baking tray with aluminium foil or a baking paper and grease with a little oil. Place the *piroshkis* on the tray, brush the tops with oil and cook in the preheated oven for about 25 minutes. They should be golden and crisp.
- Enjoy them warm, or freeze and reheat later.

Serve with sour cream or Greek yoghurt.

Zeytoon Parvardeh

زیتون پرورده

T HE BEST zeytoon *(olive)* زیتون *in Iran comes from the north, alongside the Caspian Sea. Iranians are very proud of their high-quality olives and olive oils, harvested on Mazandaran and Gilan farms. We make different kinds of dishes using olives, including zeytoon parvardeh.*

During the Iran–Iraq war, the safest places were in the northern provinces of Iran. Mazandaran and Gilan were far from the bombs and missiles. Unlike many other Iranian families, my family never moved there for good.

My parents liked to travel once a year to the sea in the summertime for our family holiday. I still remember those summers. We used to rent a villa with my dad's brother and his family. My cousins were a few years younger than us, but we got along well.

It was about six hours' drive from Tehran to Mazandaran and the town of Khezer Shahr خزر شهر. The villa was spacious, with enough bedrooms for all of us. The rough, white plaster walls, wooden floors and ceilings were typical of the villas in Khezer Shahr. The garden of each villa was separated from the one next door by low plants and decorative palm trees and there was a barbecue in each front garden. I would stare for hours at the magnolias with their large, white flowers. The air was humid and smelled of garlic and the sea.

That summer I was 12. It was a typical hot and humid day, and I had to wear a long *mantua* and head scarf in the sticky weather. The beach for female swimming was separate from the males' and the Islamic moral police were everywhere. We had to cover our hair and bodies to avoid getting into arguments with them. I could see women in the sea swimming with all their clothes on. It feels terrible to have wet, heavy fabric sticking to your body while swimming, but they didn't have any choice if they wanted to swim in the sea with their families. I hated the beaches in Iran. Why could I not wear my bikini and swim along with my dad and my cousins?

Later in the afternoon, my family and I were chatting and walking happily towards a local outdoor food market to buy some *zeytoon parvardeh* and pickled garlic as side dishes for the barbecued meat we were going to have for dinner. These side dishes are essential in northern communities. The dinner table isn't complete without olives and pickles.

While we were walking, my mum's scarf slid down to her shoulders, and two young, bearded men in dark-green uniforms approached. They were from the moral police, the *Basij*. I was scared and thought something terrible was going to happen. As the men came closer, they shouted at my mum to cover her hair. 'You should be ashamed of yourself. We carried out the Islamic Revolution for what? You must respect the blood of martyrs in the war.'

I was worried that they were going to arrest my mum and take her to jail. My heart was racing out of panic and fear. My dad and my uncle were very apologetic, begging the *Basij* to forgive us.

The argument continued for about half an hour before they let us go. We went home without buying *zeytoon parvardeh* from the market. We were upset but at the same time glad that the argument didn't go further. My mum could easily have been put in jail for not wearing the proper hijab in those days. Later, when I was older, I was arrested twice for the same thing. I finally understood the embarrassment and humiliation my mum must have felt that day.

The conversation over dinner that night was all about how the conservative religious people in power were ruining the country. The adults urged us to obey their fanatical rules just to avoid running into serious problems. I wished I had the power to put the moral police behind bars. To this day, I still feel afraid when I see someone in a dark-green outfit as they remind me of the Iranian moral police.

We ate our dinner without *zeytoon parvardeh* but we enjoyed each other's company and the warmth of family. Though it would be impossible to return to that dinner table in Khezer Shahr today, when I look back, I see how precious it was to have my family all together that night.

Zeytoon Parvardeh

Zeytoon parvardeh is simply marinated olives.

This recipe makes enough to fill a 1 litre jar

INGREDIENTS

- 200g walnuts
- 500g pitted green olives
- 1 tbsp marjoram
- 1 pomegranate, seeded
- 2 tbsp Persian pomegranate paste
- 2 tbsp olive oil
- 2 tbsp freshly chopped mint

METHOD

- Finely grind the walnuts in a blender.
- Add all the ingredients to a mixing bowl, and, using a spoon or clean hands, mix well.
- Transfer the mixture to a clean, dry, 1 litre glass jar, and press down.
- Store the *Zeytoon parvardeh* in the refrigerator. It can be eaten immediately or for up to a month.

Serve with a cheese platter, tapas or any red meat dish.

Sosis Bandari

سوسیس بندری

Sosis *is a Farsi word for 'sausages' and* bandari *means 'port'. Sosis bandari is a dish from the south of Iran, popular as street food, and is usually eaten with bread. Food from the south is often spicy and fatty compared to food from the north of Iran. I remember they used to serve it in the main restaurant in Dizin ski resort – it was a special treat in the cold winter weather.*

I was seven when I went skiing with my dad for the first time. It was freezing cold in the Alborz mountains. My hands were numb, my nose was running non-stop and my legs were aching. It took me a long time to start enjoying skiing with my dad.

My dad has always been my hero. He was a very handsome but serious and quiet man. I remember him coming home every afternoon from work and, most days, he would bring a book back for us. I couldn't read but my older sister would read them while I would look at the pictures and ask her to tell me the stories. Sometimes I would write notes in the books with a red pen, just messy lines and shapes. I used to add my own drawings to complete the stories, which upset my sister. In our house, there was a huge library that belonged to my dad. He had many books in Farsi and English and I wanted to read them all. There were even some books in English about how to ski well, with illustrations and images. Once a week my sisters and I would sit around the dining table with my dad for our English lessons. He had very old-fashioned English books, and I would feel stupid as everything seemed so difficult. My older sister was the clever one; I was the one who got bored easily.

My dad was an accomplished skier and went to Dizin ski resort twice a week during the winter. He patiently taught my sisters and me how to ski. Later, when I could ski well, at the age of 15 or so, the biggest treat was to stop midway down the slope and buy *sosis bandari* سوسیس بندری. The sausages were fat and round, made of beef and probably lots of soya and artificial flavours. Iranian sausages are very different from the Irish ones, not so soft and mushy. They were served on a plastic plate with steam rising from them, and they were the best food in that cold and brisk weather. The steam, the smell and colour of the red sausages, and the spiciness of the dish made us feel warm, full and happy.

My dad didn't like it, though. He was a fan of homemade healthy food. He would prepare sandwiches the night before ski days and make us eat them in the cable car. He believed a real skier shouldn't waste time resting and eating. But my sisters and I always wanted the port-style sausage treats, so we would say we had a sore knee or frozen hands and that we needed to sit down in a warm place for lunch rather than eating in the cable car. It didn't happen every time, but maybe once a month, after begging my dad, he would relent and stop to buy us the dish.

This also gave me a chance to take a peek at all the handsome boys in their ski gear. Sometimes, when my dad went to the bathroom, a boy would come over to pass me his phone number. My heart would beat faster, as if I was committing a crime. With mixed feelings of excitement and fear, I would laugh and say, 'Go away! My dad is with me. He might show up any moment!' And the boys would have to quickly write their numbers down on a piece of paper or whisper them into my ear for me to remember.

I can still picture that huge restaurant in the middle of Dizin ski resort, the smell of sausages and the noise of people walking about in their ski boots on the rough stone and metal floor. I can see us sitting around a simple plastic table in the restaurant, eating our port-style sausage while looking at the beautiful sunshine and white snow through the restaurant's large windows.

Sosis Bandari

This is my own twist on the recipe for sosis bandari, or port-style sausages.

Serves 4

INGREDIENTS

- 2 medium onions
- 3 tbsp olive oil
- 1 large potato
- 2 tbsp tomato purée
- 250ml boiling water
- 100g chorizo, sliced
- 500g sausages, sliced (any kind of hard sausages are fine but soft Irish sausages are not suitable)
- 1 beef stock cube
- 1 tsp paprika powder (any kind is fine)
- 1 tsp turmeric
- 1 tsp chilli powder (as spicy as you like)
- A bunch of fresh parsley

METHOD

- Thinly slice the onions into half-moon shapes
- In a large frying pan, dry fry the onions over a medium heat for 5 minutes.
- Add the olive oil to the pan and coat the onions well.
- Chop the potato into cubes of about 2cm and add to the onion. Stir and lower the heat.
- Add the tomato purée and 250ml of boiling water and stir well.
- Add the sliced chorizo and sausages and stir well.
- Dissolve the beef stock cube in a little water and add to the mixture.
- Cover the pot and let the mixture simmer for about 10 to 15 minutes. Stir and check to see if the potatoes are cooked through.
- Add all the spices and stir well.
- When the potatoes are cooked, it's ready to serve. The sauce should be thick, not watery.

Serve with freshly chopped parsley and any kind of bread you like.

Ab Doogh Khiar

آب دوغ خیار

Ab doogh khiar *(water, yoghurt, cucumber) is a Persian cold soup and a nutritious dish for hot summer days. When I was a child, my aunt would often make* ab doogh khiar *for us. It was her specialty, her favourite dish. She would carefully chop all the ingredients – enough to feed 20 people – and mix them in a large bowl. I still remember the smell of fresh mint and cucumber in my aunt's bright and beautiful house.*

My grandmother organised family lunches and dinners often when I was growing up, and *ab doogh khiar* was one of the special dishes she and my aunt would make. My sisters and I would dance at these gatherings as my uncle played the santoor in the middle of my grandmother's huge dining room. My dad and my aunt would sing traditional Iranian songs and there would be many tears and emotional responses. The songs were mostly about love, sorrow and mystical experiences.

I thought my aunt was the most beautiful woman I had ever seen. She was slim, with long, thick, black hair. She had beautiful hands with long fingers tipped with red nail polish, and an amazing singing voice. To my sisters and me, she looked like a Hollywood actress.

I was about seven years old when my aunt got married for the second time. She had divorced her first husband, who I didn't remember, a few years earlier, and no one talked about why they got divorced, though in my family divorce wasn't a big deal. She'd had lots of boyfriends since then and we had met them all, as she had been living upstairs with my grandmother. This latest boyfriend, also embarking on his second marriage, tried hard to make friends with my sisters and me. I wasn't sure if I liked him. After all, he was going to take her away from us.

On the day of the wedding, I got up early and asked my mum's permission to go upstairs with my two sisters to witness every moment of the bride's preparation process. We lived on the first floor, while my uncle and his wife stayed on the third floor. It was a summer day, sunlight was everywhere. My aunt had big hair rollers all over her head. I could smell her perfume in the air, a sweet flowery scent. She was softly singing, almost whispering, while painting her nails red.

My uncles and cousins were coming and going, preparing for the party,

while my grandma was busy making my aunt's favourite dish, *ab doogh khiar*, for lunch. My grandma wore a simple black velvet dress with a black silk scarf and a gold ring with a large brown agate stone that she kept for special occasions.

Later, at the party, my aunt sang with my dad and my uncles played santoor. The party wasn't big, but I remember it being warm and full of singing and dancing.

My aunt moved with her husband to a beautiful house in a trendy street in the north of Tehran. The house was large and modern, full of green plants. Sometimes my sisters and I would go there to stay overnight and she would make us *ab doogh khiar*. We loved going there because they had a video player, a cordless phone and a Yamaha piano, things we didn't have at our house.

My aunt and her husband moved to California for good in the middle of her first pregnancy, and my parents bought her piano for me and my sisters. She only came back once, with her daughter and son when they were teenagers. My family were still in the same house, and my aunt and her children stayed in my grandma's house upstairs during their stay.

In 2013 I went to America with my Irish husband to meet my sisters, and we visited my aunt and her family in Los Angeles. Her house was as beautiful as her house in Tehran had been. Her daughter and son were grown up, and her husband looked much older than before. My aunt had her beautiful silver jewellery on her lovely hands as always, and that thick hair.

'What would you like me to cook for you?' she asked.

Of course my answer was *ab doogh khiar*. While she was chopping cucumbers, walnuts and herbs we talked. Although she was smiling, she looked sad and distant. She told me she cooked Persian food every day and listened to Persian songs, but had not sung since leaving Tehran. She kept herself busy in her garden and didn't look at old family photos. I could see her eyes filling with tears and she avoided making conversation about the past and family gatherings.

Every year, I have a short conversation with my aunt on 21 March, Persian New Year, and we wish each other the best for the coming year. And anytime I make *ab doogh khiar*, I think about her, about the Islamic Revolution, about families falling apart and times together becoming faint memories.

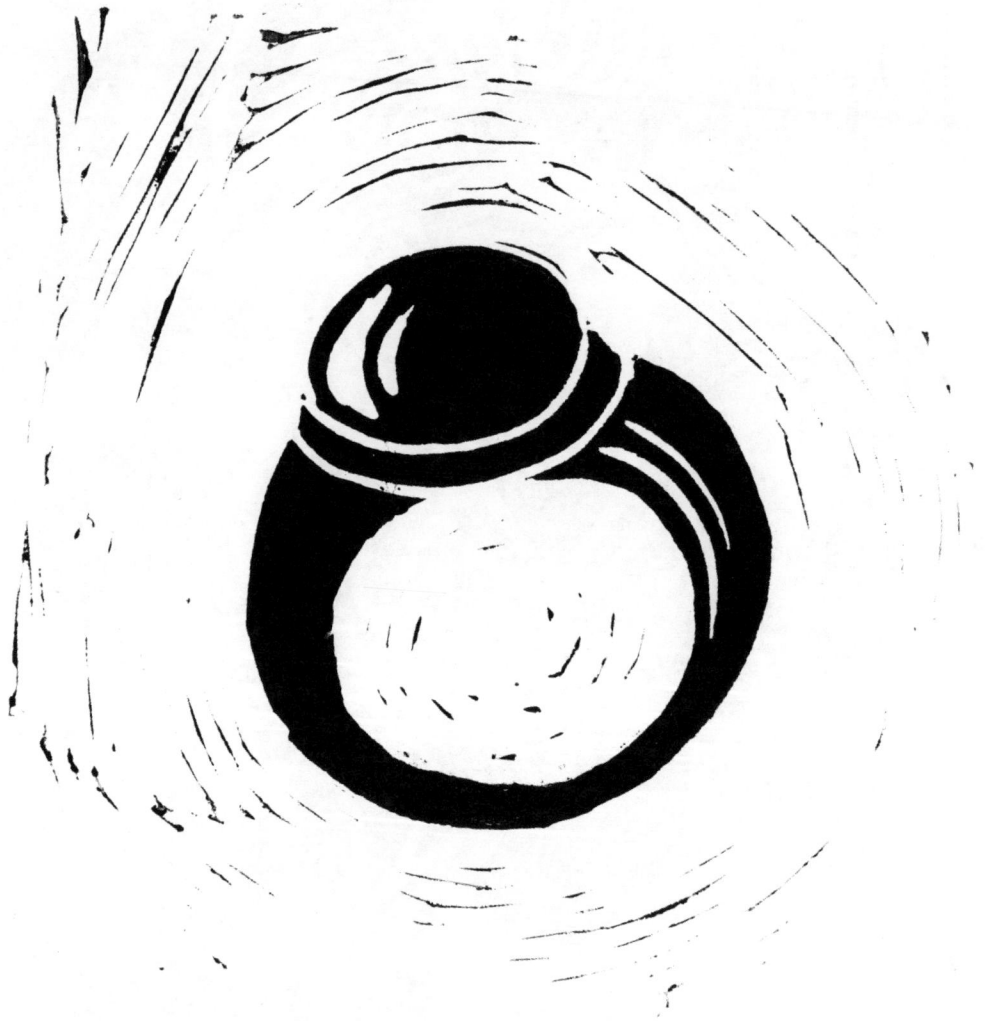

Ab Doogh Khiar

Ab Doogh Khiar is a refreshing cold yoghurt soup with cucumbers, herbs, raisins, walnuts, pine nuts and a sprinkling of dried rose petals.

Serves 6–8

INGREDIENTS

- 500g full-fat Greek yoghurt
- 5 tbsp cream
- 150ml water
- Salt and pepper
- 100g mixed fresh herbs (dill, mint, parsley and tarragon), finely chopped
- 150g chopped radish
- 150g mixed raisins and sultana mix
- 250g finely chopped cucumber (small cucumbers taste much better than large ones)
- 100g walnuts, finely chopped
- 100g pine nuts, finely chopped
- Pieces of dried bread or croutons
- A few dried edible rose petals

METHOD

- In a mixing bowl, combine the yoghurt with the cream and water. Season with salt and pepper.
- Add the rest of the ingredients except the croutons and rose petals and stir well.
- Sprinkle the croutons and rose petals over the mixture and add a few ice cubes if you like.

Serve with your favourite bread.

Kookoo Sabzi

کوکو سبزی

*S*ABZ *in Farsi means 'green' and* sabzi *is the word used for any kind of green herbs. In Iran we have different kinds of* kookoo, *which means 'frittata': eggs with mashed vegetables and sometimes meat. My favourite* kookoo *is* kookoo sabzi, *an essential dish on the Persian New Year's dinner table. I like to serve it with fresh cherry tomatoes, Persian yoghurt and flatbread.*

The main dish we eat on Persian New Year's Eve is fish with green herbed rice. Any kind of white fish works and the rice is cooked with lots of fresh herbs and garlic. Along with this, we serve some delicious side dishes such as *sabzi, torshi,* salad and sometimes *dolmeh barge mo.* The more green colours there are on the dinner table, the better.

Norooz is the most important Iranian tradition and dates back thousands of years. It is a Zoroastrian Persian tradition that survived even after the Arab invasion in the seventh century. We all are very proud of *Norooz* and this festival, it is part of our identity and distinguishes Persian culture from Arab culture. With our Indo-European roots, we celebrate *Norooz* in Iran, Tajikistan, Azerbaijan, Afghanistan and some countries in Central Asia.

Norooz falls on 20 or 21 March every year. We use the Persian calendar, which is different from the European one, and our new year starts on the first day of spring. We set a table called *Haft Seen,* which means seven items starting with the letter *s.* Each of the items has a meaning and symbolises something such as health, long life, happiness, luck and wealth. We also grow some grass from lentil or wheat seeds at home and put the newly sprouted grass on the *Haft Seen* table. There is a *Haft Seen* table set in every Iranian house for 13 days starting from 20 or 21 March. We exchange gifts and visit older relatives over the 13 days. It's very similar to the traditions of the Christmas tree and gift-giving in the Christian tradition.

On the thirteenth day, we roll up the *Haft Seen* table and *sabzeh*, the home-grown grass. We believe all families should spend the thirteenth day after New Year's Day in nature or they risk inviting bad luck for the whole year.

I remember those days when we were kids and couldn't wait for the Eid shopping, to wear our new clothes and sit around the *Haft Seen* table: eyes closed, making a wish, waiting to hear the special burst of sound from the radio or TV. It sounded like a firecracker pop, immediately followed by a traditional tune played with a kettledrum and *sorna* (Persian horn). After that, we would kiss and hug and wish each other happy New Year. My parents would give us our *Norooz* gifts. My sisters and I would have bought a book for my dad and perfume or a T-shirt for my mum with our pocket money. Afterwards, we would happily eat the sweets, or *shirini*, that my mum had made weeks before *Norooz,* with some tea.

Today I set a small *Haft Seen* table in the corner of my flat in Dublin. I don't know where my sisters or parents are when I hear the burst of sound that marks the start of *Norooz*, as we all listen out for it in different time zones across Ireland, Iran and the United States. It has been more than 17 years since I celebrated *Norooz* with my family as we are now scattered around different parts of the world.

In traditional Persian folk stories, your wish comes true if you perform all the ceremonies properly, then tie two pieces of grass together and leave them in a river on the thirteenth day. I close my eyes and my only wish is a long, healthy and happy life for my family. Perhaps one day the Islamic Republic of Iran will become a true republic and we will be able to go back and celebrate *Norooz* together, just one more time.

Kookoo Sabzi

This is my own version of *kookoo sabzi*, Iranian herb frittata.
It's a bit different from the traditional one.

This recipe will make a large pan full, or 6 generous servings

INGREDIENTS

- 1 leek, washed and finely sliced
- 250g spinach leaves, washed and roughly chopped
- 250g mixed dried parsley, coriander and chives
- 4 garlic cloves, finely chopped
- 200g walnuts, finely chopped
- 4 large eggs, beaten
- 1/2 tsp sumac
- 1/2 tsp turmeric powder
- 1/2 tsp pepper
- 1/2 tsp salt
- 3 tbsp olive oil or rapeseed oil for frying
- To serve: Persian sour barberries (*zereshk*) زرشک, stir fried in some butter (optional)

METHOD

- Add 3 tablespoons of water to large saucepan and then add the leek and spinach. Cook/wilt over a medium heat to remove excess water. After about 15 minutes, transfer to a sieve and drain to get rid of any remaining water.

- Soak the dried herbs (parsley, coriander and chives) in boiling water for 15 minutes and sieve to remove any excess water.

- Mix the spinach, leek, herbs, walnuts and garlic in a large bowl.

- To a separate bowl, add the eggs spices, salt and pepper and beat well.

- In a non-stick frying pan, heat the oil over a medium heat until hot. Add the mixture to the pan, spreading it evenly using a spatula or wooden spoon.

- Cover the pan and allow the mixture to cook for 15 to 20 minutes.

- Flip the frittata and fry the other side over a lower heat. If flipping the whole thing proves challenging, you can cut the frittata into 4 slices and turn each one separately.

- The frittata is ready when a crust has formed on both sides. Be careful not to burn it!

Serve with some sour barberries on top and Persian yoghurt on the side.

Roxana Manouchehri is an Iranian-Irish multidisciplinary artist, writer, translator, art advisor and mentor based in Dublin. She received an MFA in fine art from the Tehran University of Art. She teaches art in universities and museums across Tehran, Seoul and Dublin, including at the Chester Beatty Museum, Hugh Lane Gallery, Irish Museum of Modern Art, Open House Dublin, Rua Red and Trinity College Dublin; and has showcased her work in more than 50 group exhibitions internationally and 17 solo exhibitions worldwide.

Roxana has translated *Non-Dubliners* by Jinoos Taghizadeh from Farsi into English (Avolon, Dublin, 2018) and *Why the Moon Travels* by Oein DeBhairduin from English/Gammon into Farsi (Nazar Publications, Tehran, 2025).

She is the recipient of a Diversity Award from the Solstice Arts Centre and the Arts Council of Ireland (2021) and an artist residency from the National Youth Council of Ireland (2022).

Roxana is a founder of Transnational Arts Ireland, a digital platform promoting intercultural artistic exchange between countries. Her ongoing research into medieval European and Persian manuscripts forms the main foundation of her practice.